SARAH WHITMAN

BOSTON
THE MERRYMOUNT PRESS
MDCCCCIIII

In the interest of creating a more extensive selection of rare historical book reprints, we have chosen to reproduce this title even though it may possibly have occasional imperfections such as missing and blurred pages, missing text, poor pictures, markings, dark backgrounds and other reproduction issues beyond our control. Because this work is culturally important, we have made it available as a part of our commitment to protecting, preserving and promoting the world's literature. Thank you for your understanding.

This is a record of the Service held in memory of Mrs. Henry Whitman, by her friends and neighbours, at the Baptist Church, Beverly Farms, on Sunday afternoon, July the seventeenth, 1904. It includes four addresses; a brief poem; and a prayer and benediction by the minister, the Reverend Clarence Strong Pond.

PRAYER

THE God of love and the God of peace, Thou that maketh Thyself real unto the children of men according to their needs, unto Thee we pray, asking for Thy presence at this hour, that while we commune with the spirit of the Holy One in prayer we may also learn by the life of one who has gone of the qualities of goodness that Thou dost require of true womanhood. We ask Thee, our Father, that all the words of the mouth shall be truly acceptable to Thee, and that every moment, every hour, and every lesson, may be consecrated to Thy service in fullest measure. In His Holy Name. Amen.

ADDRESS OF JAMES B. DOW

FRIENDS and Neighbours: We are gathered here this afternoon to pay honour to a very near and dear friend, Mrs. Henry Whitman. It is not my purpose to try to follow her into the higher walks of life, into the higher realms of literature, and art, and science, and music, and all those beautiful things. There are others here who are much more competent to do that than I; but I simply want to speak to you of what she was to us as a community and people.

I think I am correct in saying that there is not a house, and hardly a heart in this community, but felt the power of her influence and her inspiration during the years that she has lived among us; and, perhaps, in enumerating some of the things that have come to us all through her influence and energy I may mention this beautiful house in which we are gathered this afternoon. You all know quite well the typical old New England meeting-house, with its hard, harsh, and somewhat uninviting interior as well as exterior; and the time had come in the life of this community when some change had got to be made. You remember, no doubt, quite a number of you, the old chapel that stood here in the corner, and you remember the old church, good of its kind, that stood about where this building stands more than twenty years ago. The matter had been discussed as to what to do to provide facilities for church work and Sunday-school work. Committees had been appointed and plans drawn, but nothing seemed to satisfy, and the work did not proceed. So only a few years ago, as you all know, many here contributed largely to the carrying out of this work. Mr. Hoyt, who was then the pastor here, took up the work of soliciting subscriptions for the purpose of renovating or enlarging the meeting-house. He succeeded so well that the Society appointed a committee to carry out the work; and you all know very well whom we went to for counsel and advice in this matter. Many had tried and failed. We went to our friend, and calmly, quietly, but how clearly, she said, "All you have to do is to lengthen the meeting-house and put two wings on it, and you will have just exactly what you want." That was done, and here is the work as you see it. The building itself, in some form or other, somehow or other, leads us into that frame of mind, of devotion, of thoughtfulness, that is so becoming in the house of God.

Then, too, in a little larger field we may speak of her other efforts and her work for the community. As many of you know, who have helped and aided us in this work, when she came here to this village it was smaller than now. There was no library or reading-room, and very little reading matter,—no room for the people growing up, or even for the older ones. That occupied her thought, and she went to work to solve that question, and then through the aid of friends a library was started and grew, a reading-room was started and it improved; and it followed on down through a number of years, until it was amalgamated with and made a part of the Beverly Public Library, with the condition that it should remain a part of Beverly Farms. Many of you can look back and remember that inspiration many times was needed in all undertakings like that; you know how difficult it is to provide for the needs. The needs were getting larger and the thoughts consequently had to be larger, and it was very difficult sometimes to see our way clearly in keeping up the work as it was then, or enlarging it to any degree; and when she gave her thought to the matter how quietly, earnestly, strongly, persistently, she said, "We must go on; the work must go on; we cannot drop it here;" and the work did go on until it was realized.

Then let me go back a little further into the work, perhaps, of a somewhat more personal character. When she came here to live in this community she desired to have a church home, and, this being the only church, she, though not a member of this denomination, came here to worship. Not only that, but she organized a class known as the Friends' Bible Class, for the purpose of aiding and assisting the church by its work. That class has been in operation for a number of years, and only very recently, as you all know, through their instrumentality and our kind friend's, a parsonage was built over on the other street there.

Before I close I wish to say a word in regard to her work as a teacher in the Bible class. It is your privilege, many of you, to occupy positions of that kind here and elsewhere. I have been a member of a Sunday-school ever since I can remember. I have had as teachers business men, lawyers, doctors, professional men of different kinds, clergymen, and so on; yet I can honestly say I never listened to the word of God being expounded so clearly, so reasonably, and so just and right as in listening to Mrs. Whitman. Not only that, but the inspiration, the spirit, the life, which she infused into everything that she took hold of, and all the subjects she took hold of, you all recognize. You all know that by personal experience, no doubt. She could quote the words of God and make them living, moving influences, powers for good, in her gentle, persistent way. I could sit there and listen to her and enjoy them with the feelings I think that the Psalmist David had when he said, "While I mused the fire burned;" and you all remember that occasion with the two disciples, on the way down to Emmaus—feeling, perhaps, somewhat as you and I do to-day—don't you remember, after the conversation with the Master, they said to one another, "Did not our hearts burn within us, as He talked with us by the way, and opened to us the scriptures?"

Those are the feelings, my friends, that we all hold dear. We shall miss her very much; and the lesson, I suppose, that comes to you and me and every one is, whether here or in yonder city, up among the mountains or the hill-tops, by the river-side or the sea-side,—it matters not,—shall we not take up her work and carry it forward? Shall we not try to spread it abroad and make others feel that, wherever we are, and under whatever conditions we are placed, we are all God's children, and we are all moving on to the great Hereafter, where we shall meet again?

So then I leave with you the influence and the power that this heart gave us, and which binds us together, above the griefs, the troubles, and worries of life. I remember how impressed I was one day with her coming in here.

She seemed to find a resting-place here. She could lay aside the thoughts, the burdens, and the cares of the days of the week, and she could come in here and find rest and peace and consolation. So may we.

STANZAS BY MRS. JAMES B. DOW
RECITED BY MISS SARAH E. MILLER

The longest summer day throbbed on,
And when its latest hour was won
    Our friend was gone.

Our friend, said we? Nay, friend to all;
For joy or sorrow, toil or thrall,
    On her might call.

True, tender, wise, and brave was she,
This life, her soul's captivity;
    Now she is free.

The acacias sweet, with creamy flowers,
Mourn, through the languid summer hours,
    This friend of ours.

And roses fair (she was more fair)
Let fall their petals on the air
    Our grief to share.

Sweet clay, with Easter lilies crowned;
The spirit, with one glad rebound,
    Its home has found.

ADDRESS OF RICHARD C. CABOT

AS Mr. Dow was explaining just now that this is a meeting of Mrs. Whitman's neighbours—past and present—I could not help thinking how many of her neighbours are absent to-day:—Martin Brimmer, Isaac Ober, Edward Ober, Henry Lee, Edmund Larcom, Edward Hooper, Mrs. Parkman, and my mother. To these neighbours and friends of hers we must try to keep close as we attempt to voice something of what Mrs. Whitman meant to us, and if we are close to her spirit, we shall be the nearer to her friends, for they were all truly part of her.

Among the achievements of the beloved friend who has passed beyond our sight, it seems fitting that we, her neighbours, should think first of her hospitality. An achievement it was, for she was shy by nature,—painfully shy in her earlier years, and even in her maturity often hampered by transformed remnants of the early weakness. The more honour to her that, in spite of all this, she achieved that bounteous, all-embracing hospitality which we know so well. She was the very incarnation of hospitality. What better symbol of it could there be than in the entrance of her house at Beverly? You remember that it was in her thought as she planned the entrance, not only that one should find one's self in one of the living-rooms of the house the instant one crossed the threshold, but that from that threshold the fireplace, the hearthstone, with all its cluster of home association, should present a warm welcome to our eyes. "Come in," it seemed to say, and "Come in" she joyfully said to all who would enter. She counted nothing human as foreign to her, no fellow creature, and no interest of any fellow creature. To us, her neighbours, to all strangers and foreigners, to rich and poor, to old and young, "Come in," she said, and wrought the welcome into the very structure of her house as she planned it.

But the hospitality which her house symbolized had entered also into every fibre of her being. Can any of you recall a mind so hospitable? Every idea on every topic, every interest of any human being, living or dead, was welcomed by her. There were many whom she loved; there were few whom she could not love. Her mind was affirmative. She said "Yes" many times; "No" less often. Many times she consented; rarely she refused. Encouragement radiated from her like perfume.

It was owing, I think, to this deeply-rooted principle of hospitality that we found her conversant, not only with the features of her own work and the lives of her friends, but with the movements of this and of other nations, with the main currents of literature, of philosophy, and even of science, and with the life of great institutions,—Harvard, Radcliffe, and Tuskegee.

She believed deeply in work, and took her part in the working world, outside which none can safely live. She cared for women's work and for every attempt made by women through education, and through the suffrage, to raise themselves and find their place in life. She cared especially for manual work. Good workmanship, ability to express one's self with one's hands, seemed to her part of the normal development of man and woman, and in her glasswork as well as in her painting, she had mastered the technical details.

Yet these impersonal and far-reaching interests were in her marvellously combined with watchful memory for the personal details of her friends' lives. Her love followed each one of us as if she had no other care, so that each of us will recall examples like the following:

A much beloved sister of my mother died forty years ago in England. Mrs. Whitman had never known her, but on the anniversary of her death she never failed to send to my mother a wreath of ivy, and always of English ivy. Who can measure the power of a love which, in the midst of multitudinous and engrossing occupations, followed the course and phases of all our lives with tenderness so exquisite?

The story of each friend's life and of the world's life was to her a love story, and in this way she was romantic through and through,—romantic in that deep and rich sense in which Isaiah, Goethe and Browning are romantic. For the world appeared to her full of a divine mystery,—a mystery not of darkness but of light, of hope, and of the miracle of birth. Her landscapes are full of this romantic spirit, for she loved and feared the world which she depicted, and never hoped to find truth or beauty in a literal copy of what lay before her. Her hope, her faith, her love, were nowhere more convincingly manifest than in the rich idealism of her landscapes, every one of which was to me a burning experience; every one full of originality, nobility, reverence, and therefore of truth. Her friends seemed to her like a cluster of gems (we all remember her romantic fondness for gems), each with a distinctive quality, a unique beauty; on this she fixed her attention, not caring to discuss or discriminate the smaller details of personality. Of a characteristic word or deed of a friend, "That's Frances," she would say, as one might say, "That's opal." To herself, as she moved in the midst of the groups of friends that gathered so often at her house, she seemed nothing more than "the thread that binds together that cluster of gems" or "the ribbon that joins the glory of many flowers." Yet she gave the whole of herself to each one of us while we were with her, and what a marvellously sympathetic listener she was! The hospitality of her mind was no greater than the hospitality of her heart. The creative stimulus of her sympathy made our past the richer as we told it. In her presence, our hopes, our plans grew, throve, and began to acquire something of worth.

Into how many discouraged lives she has thus put courage, hope, and the flush of action. "I love to see you stretch your young strength to the old endeavour," she said; yet it was to the "old endeavour," time-worn, time-honoured, that she spurred us on. There was nothing precipitate and nothing headstrong, nothing of the fanatic in the action she inspired; for though she was hospitable even to fanatics, she brought to bear upon their dreams that strong historic consciousness, that unfailing sense of humour, which chastened her idealism, kept her sane and serene throughout, and made her no less a restful than a stimulating presence. Serenity was surely one of her greatest achievements, an achievement so perfectly won that it was hard to realize the battles of self-conquest out of which it came. Her life moved on with the majesty and restfulness of a great river. No crises or revolutions were visible. She seemed never upset, never at a loss, never in a hurry, yet accomplishing in a day a volume of work unparalleled by any man or woman among my friends. This serenity was, I believe, the fruit of her sense of Immortality. The Eternal Life was for her not only a belief about the future, but a quality of the present,—a way to live at all times.

She had high hopes for the noble art of conversation, and strove incessantly to make speech noble, poignant and true, while she never failed to note and to praise the fitting word in others. But it is in her letters, I think, that she attained her greatest power over words. Many of her letters were inspired works of art, and I count it among the greatest blessings of my life that she found the time in which to write to me. From a series of her letters, extending over more than twenty-five years, I have selected a group of passages that light up the great and perennial theme of Human Friendship, and it is with relief that I turn from my words to her own.

"The true attitude towards any person or
" group of persons is not that of a critic, nor

" a judge, nor even a spectator, but that of a
" friend. And his first duty, his first privilege
" (so it seems to me), is to make his love for
" them felt by the exercise of generosity and
" faith. Criticism there may be, but the esta-
" blishment of a relationship comes before, may
" preclude criticism,—turning the water into
" wine. I do not undertake to say how this great
" thing is to be done, but that it must be done is
" to me a leading principle; the method of Jesus
" and of Paul,—of all brothers and saviours the
" world over."
" It is not self-conquest, but self-surrender that
" holds the divinest glory of heroes. Something
" of this I understand to be the secret of that los-
" ing one's soul which Christ taught, a loss of
" one's self in others, asking for no advantage,
" making no terms." . . .
" In the intercourse of spirits there should be
" much leeway, allowance of time, room to
" move about in, because the modes of spirit-
" ual manifestation are so many and so varied
" that one must take much for granted at first,
" and afterwards sift, weigh, balance—con-
" demn it may be." . . .
" Not the thought but the life constitutes the
" realm of human activity, and that life con-
" sists of finely-tempered impulses, expressing
" themselves in finely-tempered acts. Do not

" ask of others that they should first prove to
" you the nobility of their aims. Prove yours to
" them rather; that is your opportunity,—and
" in so doing invite their souls into chambers of
" welcome, support and mutual confidence."
" You will find sympathy if you will but set
" yourself to this fine art of giving. For I must
" believe that he who will most help the soci-
" ety of which he forms a part must be able to
" perceive and to make evident the central har-
" mony, to cry out of the best in him to the best
" in others in a voice which shall quicken and
" enhance the whole mass of that 'yearning up-
" ward' that deifies our clay."
" The best of us do not stand on our merits, and
" surely the worst cannot: they are essentially
" as well as potentially what they may become,
" and one's attitude must be not one of judg-
" ment passed, but of hope and confidence ex-
" pressed; an immediate appeal to that better
" self which is somewhere in each one, and
" which it is the first privilege of intercourse to
" invoke. If you came into a company of saints,
" your attitude would really be the same as
" when you came into a company of sinners.
" You would want them to feel that your heart
" felt with their heart. Through the heights
" of achievement on one side, or through the
" abysses of failure on the other, there would

" yet be a point of meeting, of love. And here
" lies the radical difference between sympathy
" and observation: the latter perceives or un-
" derstands, while the former inspires and cre-
" ates. For of all the jewels of intercourse, no-
" thing is so great as this: that the touch of Soul
" on Soul may make a new product,—'music
" as before, but vaster.'
" To me this is a bottom principle, and one which
" counts at every level: One must act on gener-
" ous presumptions; one must impute virtue;
" one must invest the world with its own di-
" vinity, if one is going to serve the world and
" lift it higher."

"Its own divinity"—no fabrication of ours, yet needing our generous devotion for its full manifestation.

Is not this the very essence and epitome of her own life? So she lived, so death found her, full of generous hopes and noble deeds—"investing the world with its own divinity." Death was a familiar but never a haunting thought to her. She had faced it, penetrated and overcome it, and she has herself voiced so perfectly what we all feel when we face her loss that from this point on I need use no words but her own.

" You know without word of mine how truly
" I feel with you in the pain and joy through

"which you have gone in that swift passing of
"your friend from this world. In some strange,
"inexplicable way death bears such witness
"to itself that I say joy too, because one is
"aware of something new, and beautiful, and
"reassuring, when one bears another company
"through that Gate.

"It seems to me now, as the Beautiful and Dear
"go forth, as if it were not so much that they
"went away as that we also go with them a
"little space, and indeed never wholly come
"back to this world again, keeping some se-
"cret companionship with those who live with
"God.

"Yet now that she 'beckons from where the
"immortals are,' the thought of her life stirs
"the soul afresh and blows upon the embers of
"the heart, inviting not to tears but to joyful,
"high endeavour.

"All our hearts are lifted up to-day in the beau-
"tiful knowledge of this spirit's return home.
"Not death, but life more abundantly. 'No-
"thing is here for tears' except those sweet
"tears which anoint the breast and quicken
"impulse, unlocking the deeper chambers of
"the heart. And yet I know that this change is
"so great, this loss so keen,—and I send you
"the old love again, and more."

ADDRESS of THORNTON K. LOTHROP

IT seemed to me, my friends, if there was to be a memorial service anywhere for Mrs. Whitman that this was the place—here she had her home; this was the village she loved, in whose people she took so strong an interest, on whose lives and characters she had such an influence, whose counsellor and friend she was for many years. It is only natural that you should wish to pay a tribute to the memory of a woman who shared your joys and sorrows, lightened your burdens and troubles, and who was always ready to answer your every call. No memorial could be more grateful to her than this meeting, and the feeling which prompted and inspires it.

She first came here for the summer some thirty years ago, and, though she has been here ever since, there was then no certainty that she would return; yet one might have noticed the difference between her and the ordinary summer visitor. She did not regard herself as a mere bird of passage. She began at once to try to know the men and women among whom she was passing a single season, and the interest she showed in them they were not slow to recognize. She knew by intuition how to gain the confidence and win the affection of the people about her. There was never a great grief that came to any of us that Mrs. Whitman was not the first one to come in and give us strength and comfort. There was never a great joy that she did not wish to share in it. There was nothing in this village in which Mrs. Whitman did not take part. She was always of you, and among you.

Almost immediately on coming here she began a Bible class which met every Sunday after the morning service. This was continued during her life, and it is not too much to say that every one who was at any time a member of that class loved her with devotion, sincerely mourns her to-day, and will always cherish the remembrance of her as a most precious possession. She had for more than thirty years a similar class at Trinity Church in Boston during the winter, and your sorrow here finds its counterpart in those who were her scholars there.

Dr. Cabot has spoken, and has spoken very justly, of her great faith in human nature. She regarded the needs of persons rather than their deeds. She believed in mankind; she believed that there was some divine spark in every human being, and if you could only find out what it was, and where it was, and kindle it, you might change the whole man. When somebody said to her not many months ago, "I think such a person very uninteresting," she said, "No, not uninteresting; nobody is uninteresting; you have only to get the clue that there is to everybody to find some clear, life-giving thing about him that you will be glad to know.'" It was this faith, this insight, and this sympathy that brought her into such peculiar and close personal relation with us all.

Her interests, however, were not confined to the little circle whom she could personally reach and touch. She was eager to raise the standard and broaden the field of education in this country. For Radcliffe College her labours were unceasing. She was daunted by no difficulties; and, as one of its strongest supporters has said, she carried that college on her shoulders for many years. She was also keenly alive to the educational needs of our Southern people, both white and coloured. She was a worker for and a liberal contributor to Booker Washington's school at Tuskegee. She was no less a warm friend of the Industrial College at Berea, Kentucky, for both white and coloured people; and by her will she has eased for those who come after her the management of both these institutions. There are many other charities that will much miss her sympathy and her open purse. She had a method in her dealings with all such as appealed to her, and their wants, their condition, their purposes, their proper aims and policies were all separately pigeon-holed and docketed in her mind and often in her desk.

But perhaps her greatest public work was for the Museum of Fine Arts in Boston. She was never a trustee of that institution; she had no connection with it officially, but she gave to it time, strength, thought, and counsel,—all that she could have given had she been the person solely responsible for its management and prosperity. She was the right hand of its presidents, the confidential adviser of its trustees, who went to her again and again upon questions of doubt or difficulty when they wanted good advice; she never failed them, and the Museum and its Art School owe to her to-day as much as to any living person. It was not merely what she did for them directly, but what she did indirectly. Her influence with the community was great, and her friends contributed to and aided her in the Museum's support and growth. Indeed there was no undertaking for the public good in which she could do any service that she was not ready to do it. She laboured with all her strength; she exhausted her vitality; she gave up her life, in fact, to the calls of her friends, to the calls of the public, and to the calls of her work of all kinds.

She was a woman of rare intellectual gifts,

and was most appreciative of these gifts in others; a person of most versatile powers and varied interests, possessing great artistic taste and feeling, and a very high degree of artistic capacity and skill. Whether she were a great artist it is not for me to say, but that she was a growing artist no person who has seen and compared her earlier with her later work would doubt for a moment.

No one who ever knew Mrs. Whitman can separate her work as an artist from her personality; can distinguish between what she did and what she was. Her friends by no means agree as to where her best work may be found. Some of them prefer her landscapes, and others think her permanent reputation lay in her glass; but it seems to me that her portraits show the greatest advance both in technical skill and in spirituality. There is one among them which is not merely a superficial likeness, but the counterfeit presentment of the man, and there is a charm or quality in it which I have rarely seen in any picture, and which would do credit to any artist.

Her great gifts she used greatly, to noble ends; her aims and purposes were high; her ambitions were worthy of her nature; and for the causes she believed in, the friends whom she loved, indeed for every one who needed her, she was ready to work with a disinterestedness, a forgetfulness and disregard of self, and a devotion and perseverance such as she symbolized in the three figures of Love, Patience, and Courage in the window now at St. Louis, which was her last great work.

Her life was rich and full—full to the end; rich in high aspirations and successful achievements; rich in the love she gave and in the love she received; rich in the widespread as well as penetrating influence which she exerted, not only on those who came nearest to her, but on the community in which she lived.

ADDRESS OF MR. JUSTICE HOLMES

MY Friends and Neighbours: I shall say but a very few words, and those a repetition of what already has been said better, in memory of the friend and neighbour whom we have lost, — a woman, and therefore to be mentioned with the delicacy and reserve which are her right as a woman, but worthy of public honour, and not to drop into silence without loving praise.

We are not likely to see another memorial meeting in which so many of those who are present feel the sting of personal loss; for she was a friend and neighbour to us all. She had the power which some large natures possess of getting on to terms with almost any one and bringing out the best that was in him. That means, of course, that beside a liberal sympathy, she had an alert and open mind,—a mind more ready than most to appreciate all varieties of character and gift. Her experience in the studio had given her a large command of the unfamiliar observations and sayings of those who look on the world at first hand and draw what they tell us, not from literature, but from life. At the same time she was intimate with philosophers, who stand at the pole opposite to art. She had taken part alike in the administration of public charities and of the higher education of her sex. She was a favourite and a leader in society. I might go on accumulating the varied experiences which united to make her companionship interesting as well as delightful to people who had nothing in common except their love for her. And it was done so easily—always with a smile, often with a laugh, which she so readily could command that it almost made an amusement out of the interchange of high thoughts. She had her full share of intimacies with the distinguished, but it is more charming to remember by what troops of younger people she was adored.

I called her friend and neighbour. "Neighbour"—I think she loved the word. I think those who have spoken before me have noticed the same thing, and I say that she was our neighbour as the Samaritan was neighbour in the parable. If any of us was sick or sorry, when did she fail to divine it and in some way put herself to silent trouble, to help us if she could, to show her sympathy if she could do no more? How many a shy youth found in her house his first glimpse of the great world of which he had dreamed, until then in vain.

It seems to me that the social difficulties of our time are even more sentimental than economic, and that those who let their democratic feeling grow cold, be they rich or poor, do more than any others to shake the present order of things. If I am right, a woman who meets her kind with Mrs. Whitman's sympathy, with Mrs. Whitman's democracy of soul, is, on the other hand, a pillar and a bond to uphold and to unite the Commonwealth. I think the first and also the last thing to say of her is that she was generous of herself to all, and that in being so she made the greatest gift, the greatest contribution, that she could make, that any one can make, to keep society together and alive.

Generosity, intelligence, humour and love —a noble combination—and to these must be added the high courage of her end. Already the lilies under which she was borne down the aisle of Trinity have drooped their white trumpets. The house she built, after the image of her hospitable soul, by the neighbouring beach, is an empty shell, which soon will cease to echo of its past. The great silence is descending. But the hearts, the many hearts in which she truly lived, will whisper of her until they too are no more; and even then, and for cycles still to come, the impulse of her goodness will reverberate in souls that knew her not, and your grandchildren will be better because she aspired and loved and endured.

BENEDICTION

AND now may the peace of God, which passeth all understanding, keep your hearts and minds through Christ Jesus; and may the blessing of God the Father, the friendship of the Son, and the spirit of the Holy One of Israel rest upon you, now and for evermore. Amen.

Printed by Libri Plureos GmbH in Hamburg, Germany